MOUNTAIN MAZES

Roger Moreau

Sterling Publishing Co., Inc.   New York

Library of Congress Cataloging-in-Publication Data

10   9   8   7   6   5   4   3   2

Published by Sterling Publishing Company, Inc.
387 Park Avenue South, New York, N.Y. 10016
© 1996 by Roger Moreau
Distributed in Canada by Sterling Publishing
% Canadian Manda Group, One Atlantic Avenue, Suite 105
Toronto, Ontario, Canada M6K 3E7
Distributed in Great Britain and Europe by Cassell PLC
Wellington House, 125 Strand, London WC2R 0BB, England
Distributed in Australia by Capricorn Link (Australia) Pty Ltd.
P.O. Box 6651, Baulkham Hills, Business Centre, NSW 2153, Australia

Sterling ISBN 0-8069-6110-4

CONTENTS

A NOTE ON THE SUGGESTED USE OF THIS BOOK

As you work your way through the mazes of this book, use a pointer rather than a marker. This will enable you to take the journey over and over again and will give your friends a chance to climb the seven summits without showing them the routes you took.

Special warning: On the following climbs, avoid the temptation to start at the *end* of the trail or *top* of the mountain and work your way backwards. That technique would be a violation of the rules and could result in serious injury to any climber.

INTRODUCTION

Climbing to the top of a high mountain is challenging, but also exhilarating and rewarding. During the second half of the twentieth century, mountain climbing has become increasingly popular. In 1953, when the British made the first ascent of Mount Everest, the highest mountain in the world, the age of mountaineering came alive. Most of the highest peaks in the world have been climbed since then. Increased emphasis on physical fitness, improved equipment and modernized modes of travel have made such quests more feasible.

In 1981, two Americans, Frank Wells and Dick Bass, set the ambitious goal of being the first to climb to the top of the highest mountain on each of the seven continents. Although these mountains had been previously conquered, no one had attempted to subdue all of the "seven summits." It was a daunting task, but in 1985, Dick Bass became the first to complete the ascent of all seven summits.

Time and expense prevent most mountaineers from journeying to each of the seven continents and climbing its highest mountain. But regardless of what factors might keep you from having such an adventure, you can climb the seven summits right here, right now. Before you go, however, you must learn the techniques of climbing and get into shape by doing the climbs on the next few pages. Learn ice climbing by climbing the Nisqually Glacier on Mount Rainier in Washington. When climbing Rainier, stay on the trail and avoid falling into the crevasses. Find a clear trail to the summit. Next, learn to rock-climb by climbing the face of El Capitan in Yosemite, California. Climb the ropes by finding a continual rope link to the summit. In some places you may have to descend a rope in order to find your way to the top. Finally, get into shape by climbing the highest mountain in the contiguous United States, 14,497-foot Mount Whitney in the High Sierras of California. Find a clear path and climb the ropes until you can reach the summit. You cannot step over any rocks and you may have to descend ropes in order to find your way.

When these practice climbs are complete, you will be ready to begin your journey to climb the seven summits. You will have to make many difficult and important decisions along the way. Just remember you will be successful if you don't give up. Good luck.

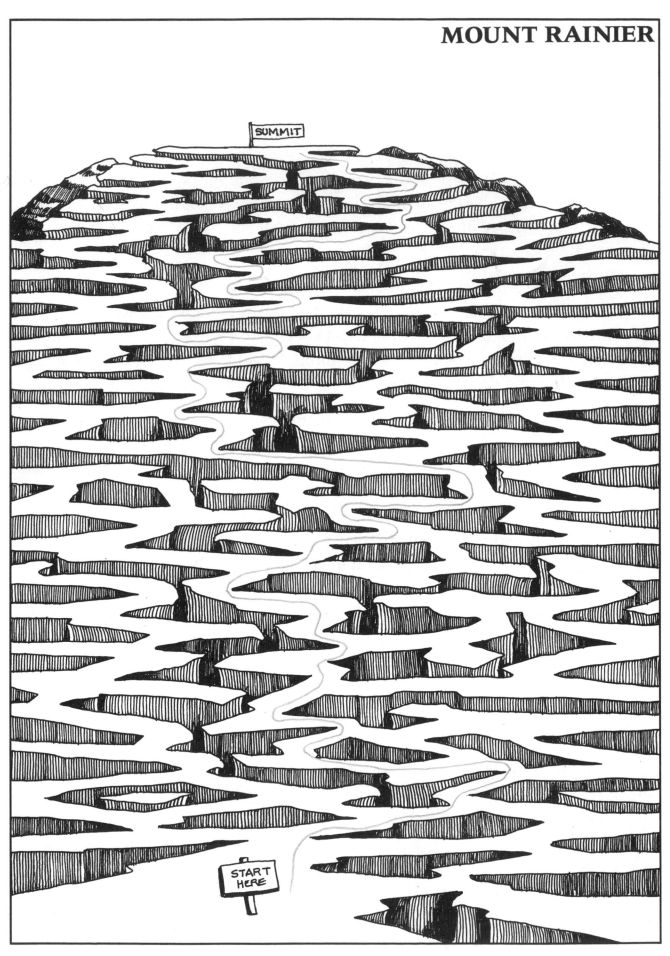

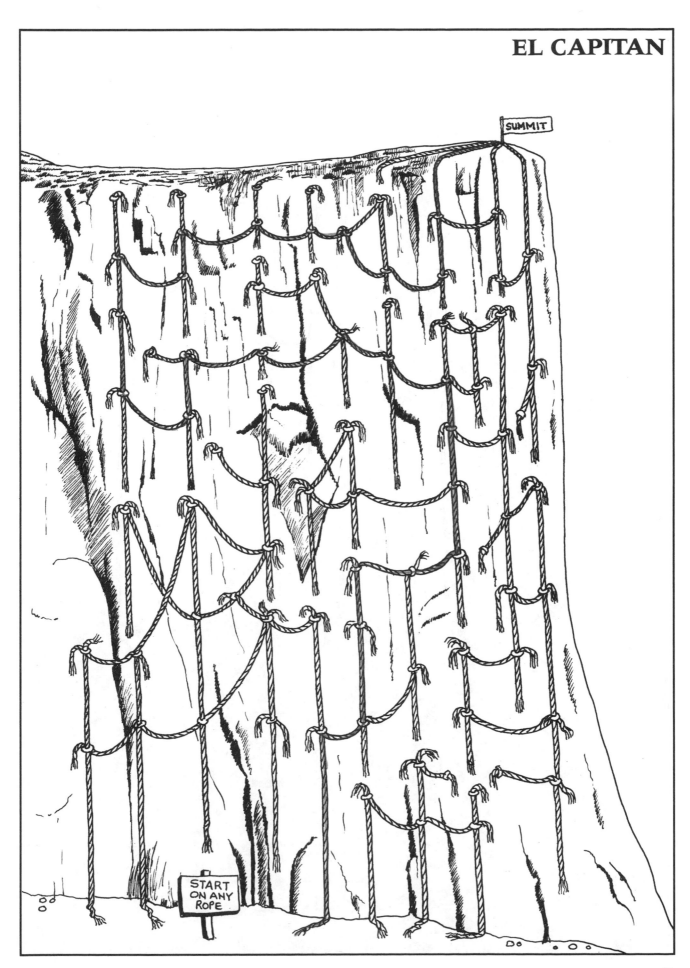

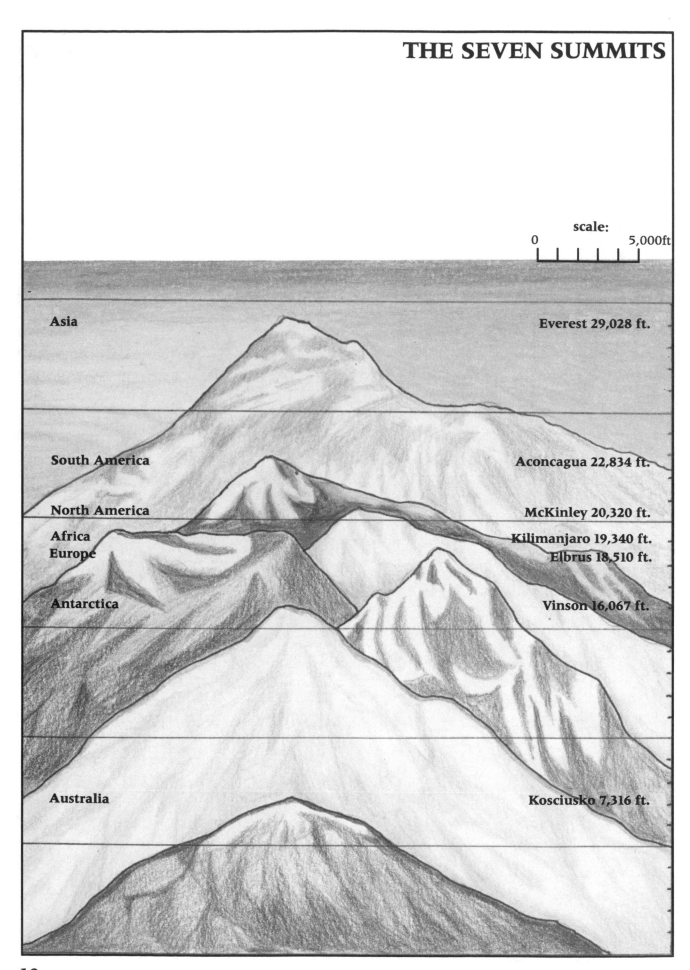

THE SEVEN SUMMITS

scale:

0   5,000ft

Asia   Everest 29,028 ft.

South America   Aconcagua 22,834 ft.

North America   McKinley 20,320 ft.

Africa   Kilimanjaro 19,340 ft.
Europe   Elbrus 18,510 ft.

Antarctica   Vinson 16,067 ft.

Australia   Kosciusko 7,316 ft.

AUSTRALIA

Australia is the smallest continent and the only continent that is a country. Because it lies entirely south of the equator, Australia is sometimes called the Land Down Under. It is low and flat except for mountains along the eastern coast and a few high areas in the interior. The highest mountain in Australia is Mount Kosciusko.

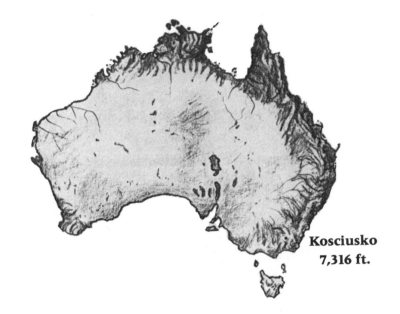

Kosciusko
7,316 ft.

MOUNT KOSCIUSKO
7,316 FEET

Mount Kosciusko is in the Muniong range of the Australian Alps in southeastern New South Wales. At 7,316 feet, this mountain is the lowest of the seven summits. Because of its height and mild terrain, it is not considered a difficult mountain to climb. Who made the first ascent is unknown. Likely the summit was reached centuries ago by some tribesmen seeking a high-vantage viewpoint.

Begin your climb at the bottom left corner. Your challenge is to find a clear pathway between the rocks to the summit. Do not step over any rocks. Take your time and have a nice hike.

Special note: Some geographers include the islands near Australia as part of the Australian continent—namely Oceania or Australasia. Included would be the island of New Guinea. The highest peak of Australasia is 16,023 foot Carstensz Pyramid on New Guinea. It was first climbed in 1936. If you prefer to climb Carstensz Pyramid rather than Kosciusko, you can make that substitution.

START HERE

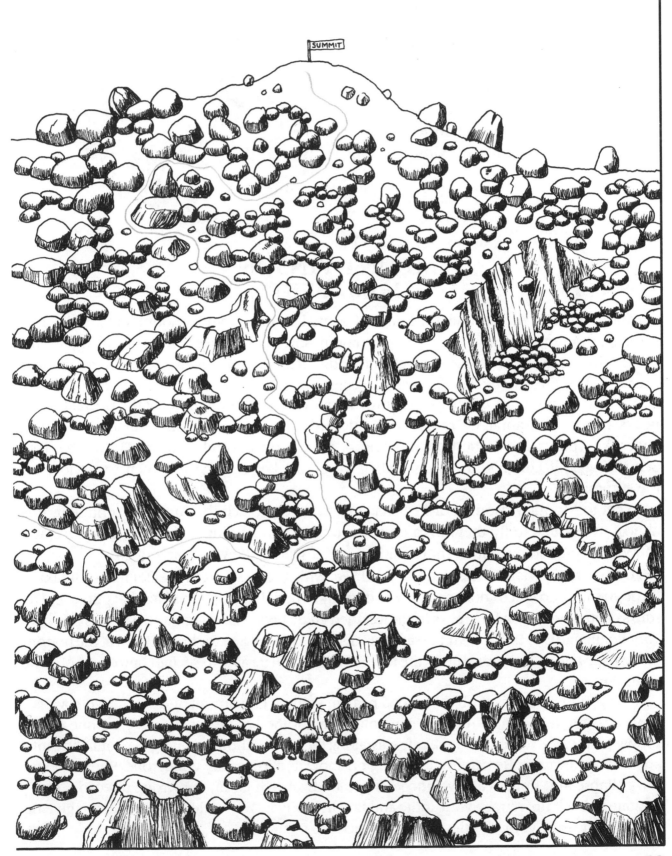

ANTARCTICA

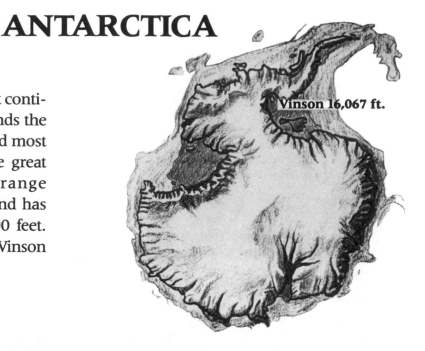

Vinson 16,067 ft.

Antarctica is the fifth-largest continent in the world and surrounds the South Pole. It is the coldest and most desolate region on earth. The great Transantarctic mountain range crosses the entire continent and has peaks rising as high as 16,000 feet. The highest of these is Mount Vinson at 16,067 feet.

MOUNT VINSON
16,067 FEET

Mount Vinson's location near the South Pole makes this a unique mountain to climb. Just getting to the mountain in such a remote and hostile environment creates challenges. This mountain is always covered with ice and snow. Temperatures below zero, icy winds and occasional "whiteouts" keep climbers in a constant struggle for survival.

In 1966, however, an American-led expedition set out to climb many of the unchallenged peaks in the Transantarctic range. They succeeded in climbing many, but their ultimate goal was Antarctica's highest peak—Vinson. Finally, on December 18, at 11:30 A.M., Pete Schoening, Bill Long, John Evans and Barry Corbet became the first men to set foot on the summit.

To get to Mount Vinson, your first challenge will be to reach the Antarctic continent. It is almost impossible to fly there because of the difficulty in landing and taking off on ice and snow. Going by ship is much more feasible, and it will be the way you will go.

The mountain is located near the Weddell Sea, which is often frozen over for miles. Breaking through the ice to reach shore can only be done by a special ship designed for that purpose. The ship's captain will look for cracks in the ice, then guide his ship through until shore is reached. Your challenge is to find a clear passage through the Weddell Sea to shore. Begin at the bottom of the page and guide your ship to the top. There you will be able to set foot onto the Antarctic continent.

Now you're ready to climb the second peak in your seven-summit quest—the ice-covered, crevasse-strewn Mount Vinson. Begin your climb at the bottom of the page on one of the snowy pathways. You must find a safe way along the path without stepping over or falling into any of the crevasses. Be careful. Climbing on snow and ice is very dangerous. Snow bridges can collapse and slopes can avalanche. If you find yourself going the wrong direction, don't hesitate to back up, retrace your route and find a new way. Your determination not to give up will pay off. Trust your abilities. You will reach the top.

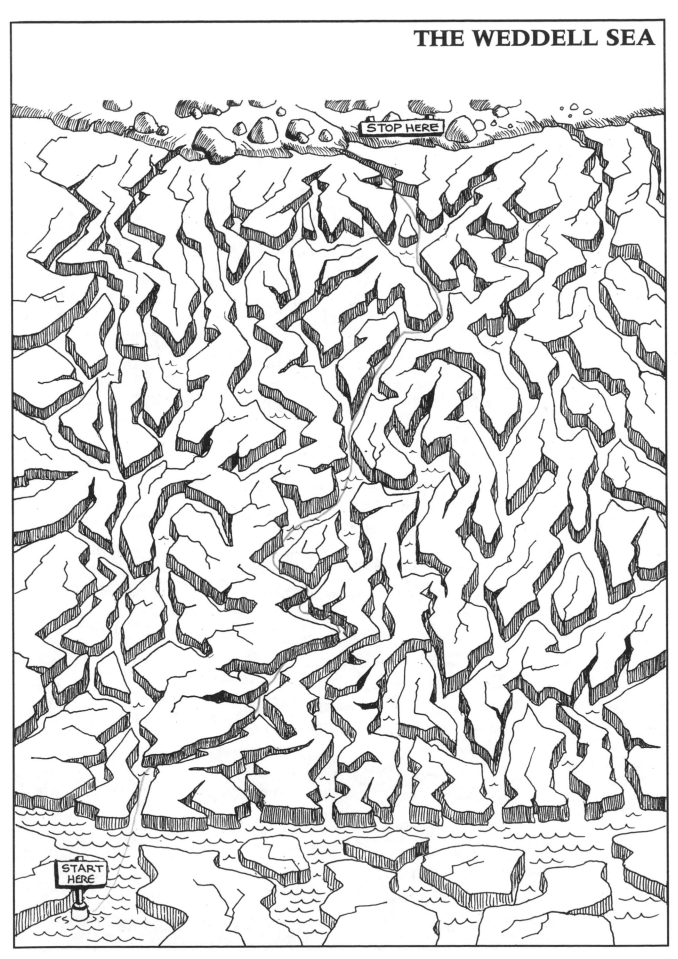

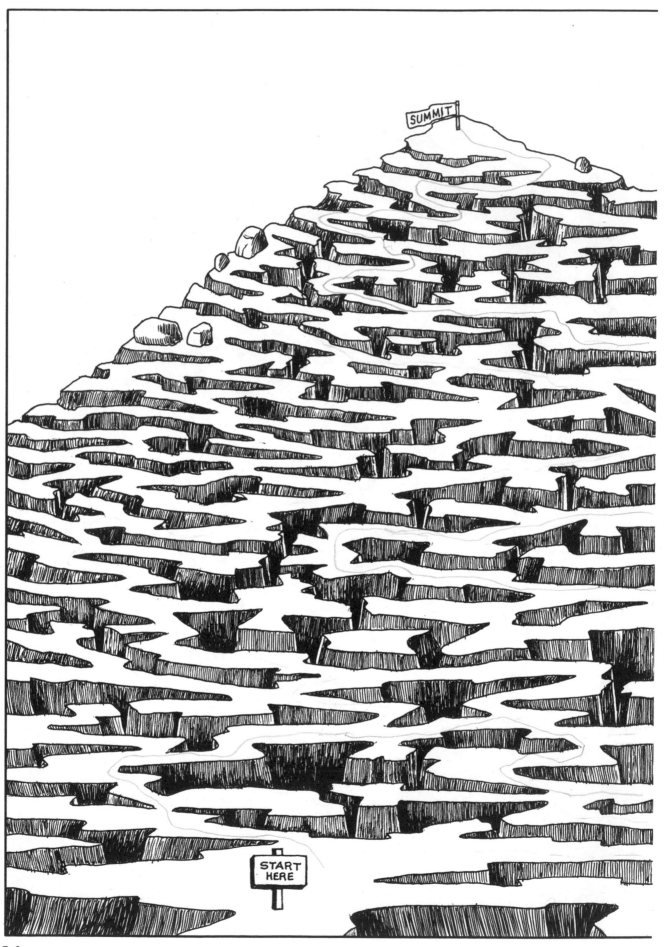

EUROPE

Europe is one of the smallest continents—only Australia is smaller. Yet it has a larger population than all of the other continents except Asia.

A series of Alpine mountain ranges traverses southern Europe. From west to east, this includes the Sierra Nevada, the Pyrenees, the Alps, the Apennines, the Carpathians, the Balkans and the Caucasus. Mount Elbrus, at 18,510 feet, is the highest mountain in Europe and is in the Caucasus.

Elbrus 18,510 ft.

MOUNT ELBRUS
18,510 FEET

Mount Elbrus is an extinct volcano. It was first climbed in 1868 by Douglas W. Freshfield. Because of its height, it is covered with snow and a number of glaciers descend from its summit. Technically, it is not considered a difficult mountain to climb. However, its high altitude can cause problems, especially if a climber ascends too fast. Oxygen gets thinner the higher the altitude, so it is important to climb slowly and to gradually acclimatize to the altitude. Otherwise, altitude sickness is a real threat—headache, nausea, lack of appetite and poor or no sleep. Freshfield experienced this during his historic first ascent of the mountain.

To get to Mount Elbrus, you must hike up the trail to the plateau at the foot of the mountain. Over the years, rocks falling from the mountain have littered the path that crosses the plateau, blocking the way. Over the years, climbers have made new paths around the rocks, but rocks continue to fall. Now there are many paths that cannot be used. Fortunately, a recent expedition cleared a path for you. You must find that path. It will not be blocked by rocks. Begin your approach from the left. Exit on the right. The mountain will be straight ahead.

Now you are ready to climb Mount Elbrus. Go slowly. This will help prevent mountain sickness. Look around carefully. This will minimize the risk of getting lost. Start your climb at the bottom left corner of the page. Your challenge is to find a clear pathway to the mountain's summit. Be careful to avoid the crevasses as you get higher on the mountain. Don't hesitate to descend and to set out in a new direction if you get off the right route. Remember, you cannot step over the rocks that are in your way; and you cannot jump over crevasses.

The conquest of Elbrus will be your third victory. You will have four to go. There are some tough climbs ahead, but if anyone can succeed, you can. Be tough!

START
HERE

AFRICA

**Kilimanjaro
19,340 ft.**

Africa is the second-largest continent in the world. It is a land of varied, scenic beauty best described in superlatives. It has the largest desert, the longest river, the longest freshwater lake, and some of the most spectacular waterfalls. The highest mountain is Kilimanjaro in Tanzania. Although it is near the equator, ice and snow cover much of it all year round.

MOUNT KILIMANJARO
19,340 FEET

Mount Kilimanjaro is a volcano with smoke still rising from its huge summit crater. It dominates the horizon as its bulk rises out of the Tanzanian lowlands. Hans Meyer and his guide, Ludwig Partscheller, were the first to reach the summit in 1889. They had no trouble keeping the mountain in view as they trekked overland to reach the mountain base. But they did have trouble with the tropical heat and the distance they had to travel. If it hadn't been for the mountain's visibility, they possibly would have given up or become lost. The only problem they had on the actual climb was the altitude, as Kilimanjaro is almost one thousand feet higher than Mount Elbrus.

You must cross the hot Tanzanian jungle to get to the base of Kilimanjaro. Begin your trek anywhere along the dirt road on the left side of the page and trek across the page to the sign. Nothing should block your way. You must find a completely clear path. Tree branches cannot block your path, and you can only cross rivers by crossing bridges. When you reach the sign, turn the page and you can begin your climb of the volcano. Again, a clear path must be found. Do not step over rocks. Your goal is the highest point on the right side of the summit.

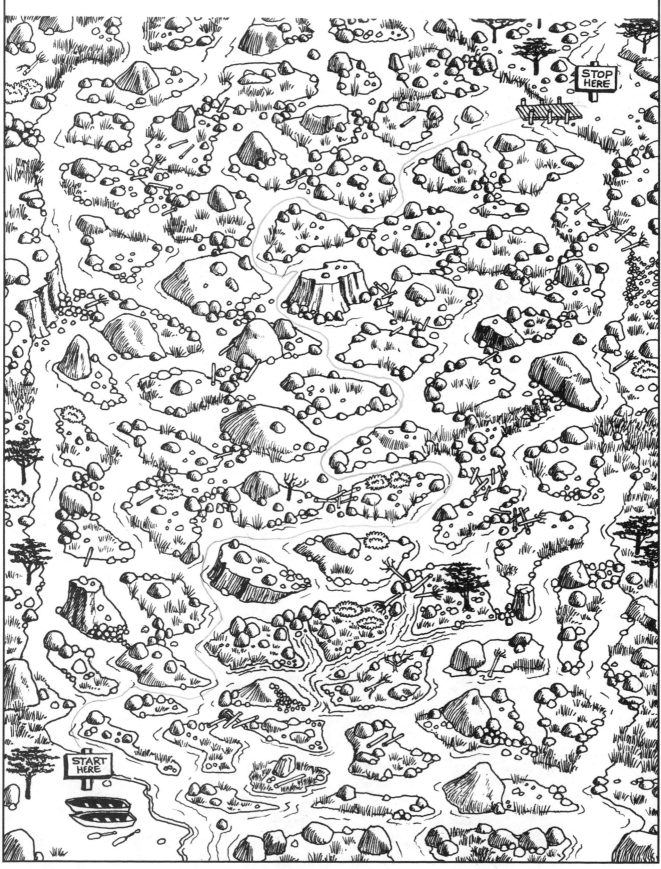

START ANYWHERE ALONG THIS ROAD.

KILIMANJARO
19,340 feet
Begin climb here.

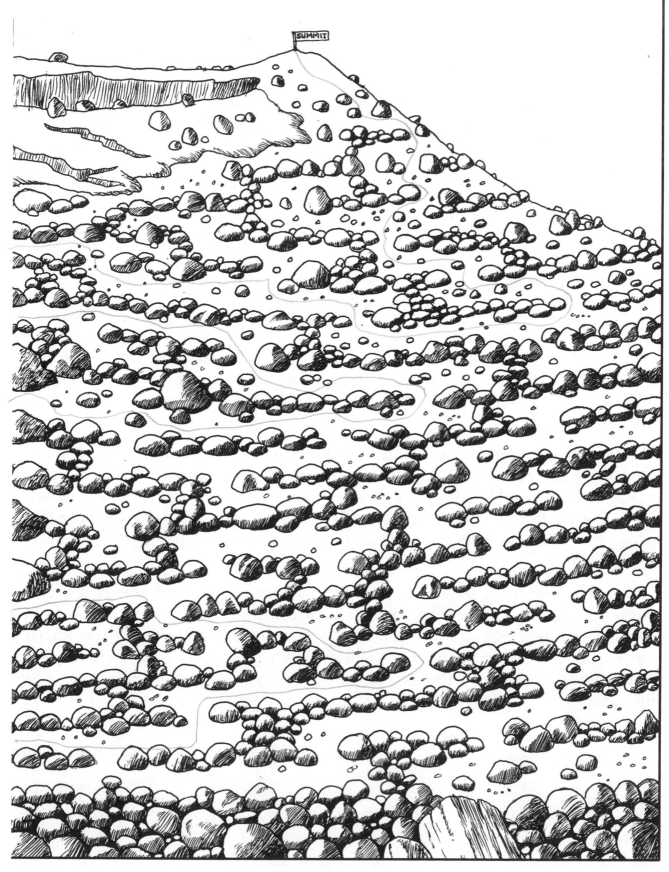

NORTH AMERICA

North America is the third-largest of the seven continents. It juts into the frigid Arctic Ocean to the north and languishes lazily in warm tropic breezes to the south. The Pacific Ocean laps along its western side and the Atlantic Ocean washes against it down its eastern side. Mount McKinley is the highest peak on the North American continent.

McKinley
20,320 ft.

MOUNT MC KINLEY
20,320 FEET

Mount McKinley is in the state of Alaska. This mountain offers danger and difficulty. Being so far north, almost within the Arctic Circle, altitude is only one consideration when climbing this mountain. Planning has to include the eventuality of extremely cold temperatures and unpredictable weather.

In 1913, Archdeacon Hudson Stuck, Harry P. Karstens and two companions were the first to climb to McKinley's summit. Many have since summited this mountain. Climbers once had to trek for weeks to reach McKinley's base. Today, within a few hours, they can be dropped off by airplane at the foot of the mountain's glaciers. The actual climb begins by ascending these dangerous glaciers until the base of the mountain itself is reached, and then up the snowy slopes and ridges to the top.

On climbs over great snowfields, where the weather can turn bad quickly and cause "whiteouts," climbers put up marker poles linked with ropes so they can find their way up and down. On the next page, the marker poles and ropes are in place. Some of the ropes have broken, but the correct route to the top is marked with an unbroken rope link from pole to pole. Start at the bottom. You must find the correct route by climbing the unbroken rope line to the summit.

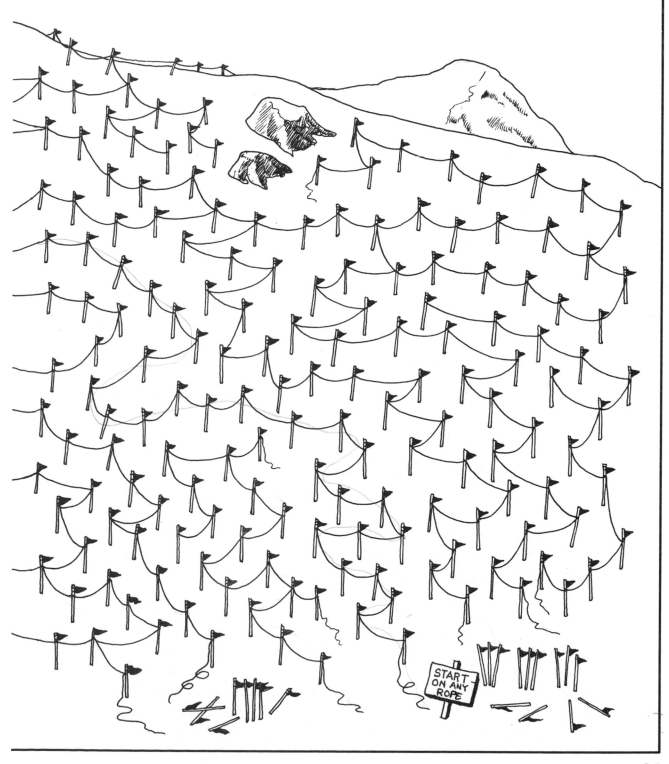

SOUTH AMERICA

South America is the fourth-largest continent. North America trails down into the northern border of South America and South America continues south to within 600 miles of Antarctica. The equator extends across the continent at almost its widest point. The great Andes Mountains extend along the entire western coast of South America.

Aconcagua 22,834 ft.

MOUNT ACONCAGUA
22,834 FEET

In the Andean mountain range of South America, more than fifty peaks rise to over 20,000 feet. Aconcagua, at 22,834 feet, is the highest peak on this continent. It is located in Argentina where the Andes brush its western edge.

Shortly before the turn of the century, a British expedition, under the leadership of Edward A. Fitzgerald, made several attempts to be the first to climb the mountain. It was Matthew Zurbriggen who arrived alone on the lofty summit January 14, 1897.

Snow and ice continually cover Aconcagua's upper slopes, but it is the high altitude that makes this peak a tough challenge. It is more than 2,500 feet higher than Mount McKinley, making Aconcagua the highest peak in the Western Hemisphere.

Getting to Aconcagua requires miles of hiking up canyons and crossing streams. It can be very dangerous and rough going. Your task is to cross the Vacas River without falling into it. Begin your crossing of the Vacas on the left side of the canyon and cross on the bridges and logs until you reach the right side of the canyon. Be careful as you go, because many bridges and logs have collapsed. If you get off-route, back up and find a new one. When you get to the other side, you will be ready to climb the mountain.

Begin your climb at the base of the mountain. Many fixed ropes are in place from previous climbs, but some ropes have broken. You must find a continual rope link that will take you to the top. You can traverse and descend if necessary to reach the top, but you cannot move onto a rope that is not connected to the one you are on. When you reach the top, you will have conquered your sixth summit. Only the mighty Mount Everest will remain for you to climb— the highest mountain in the world. It is over 6,000 feet higher than Aconcagua. But don't despair. The skills you are gaining will enable you to conquer Everest.

START ON THIS SIDE.

STOP ON THIS SIDE.

START
ON ANY
ROPE.

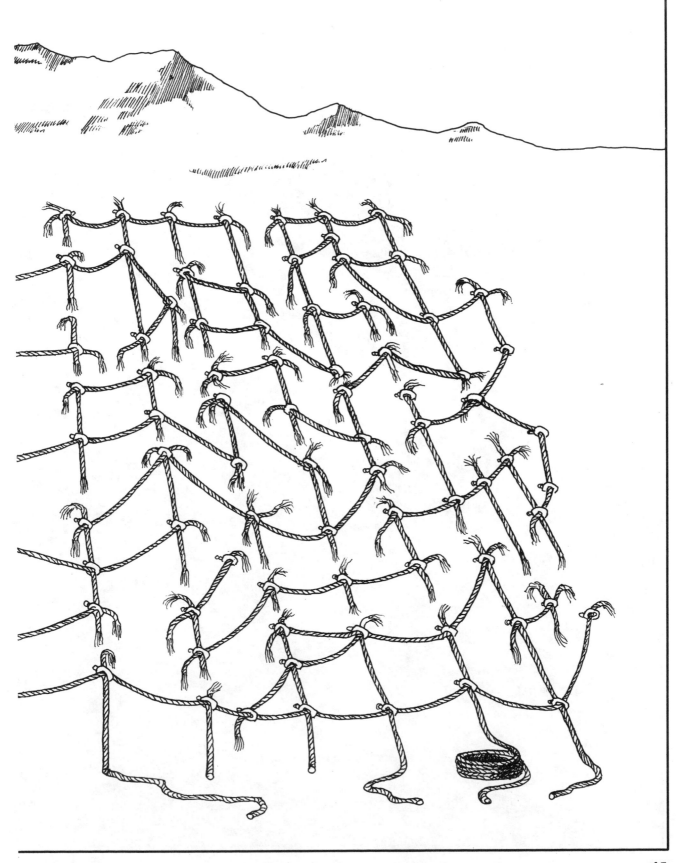

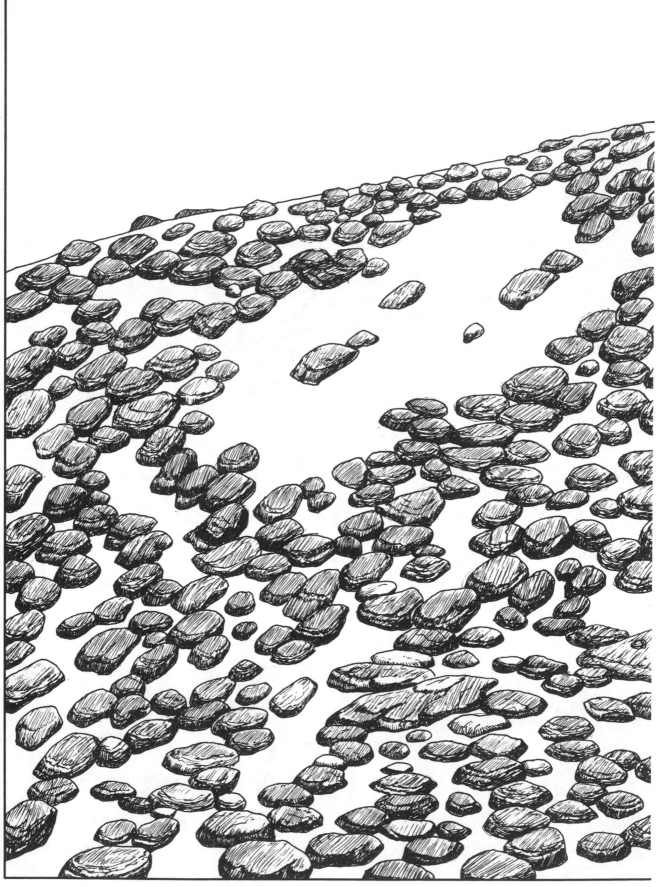

CONGRATULATIONS

You have succeeded in climbing the seven summits. The feat was not easy, but with determination, skill and courage, you have faced the challenge and been victorious. You can be numbered among the few who have achieved this lofty goal. Now go forth and face the rigors of each day with the same fine qualities that it took to climb the seven summits. May your focus be ever upward and your footsteps ever steady.

CLIMBING GUIDES

For climbers who became lost, the following pages are a climbing guide. Use the climbing guide only if necessary.

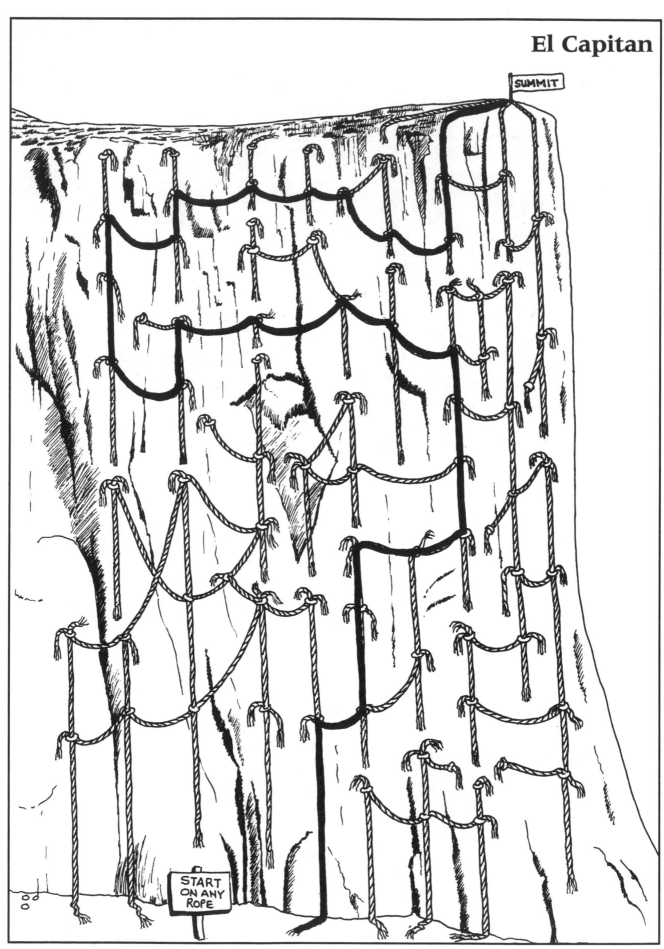

SUMMIT

START ON ANY ROPE

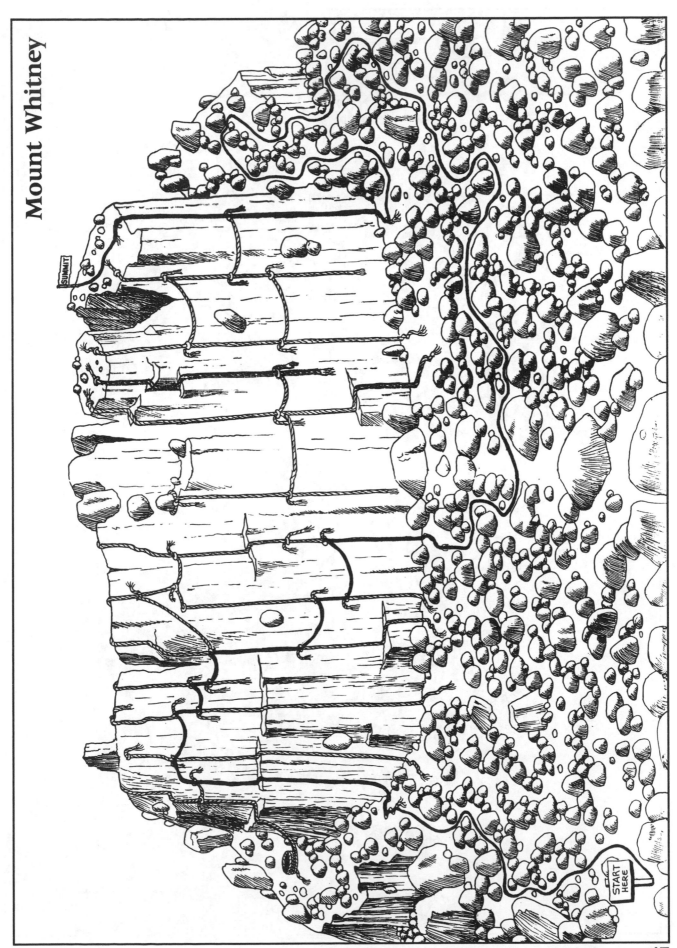

Mount Whitney

START HERE

SUMMIT

47

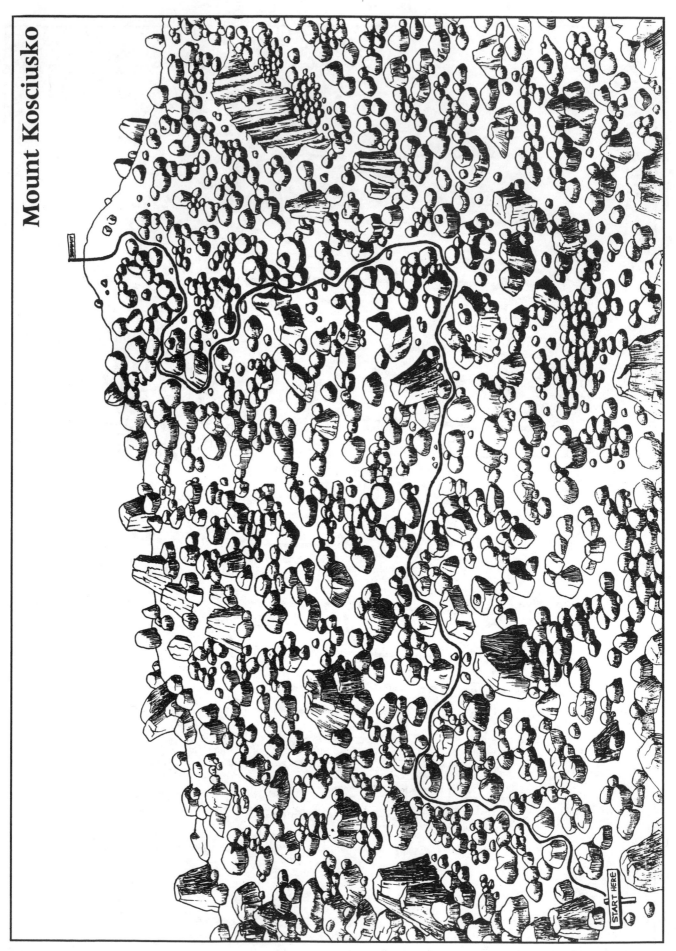

Mount Kosciusko

START HERE

48

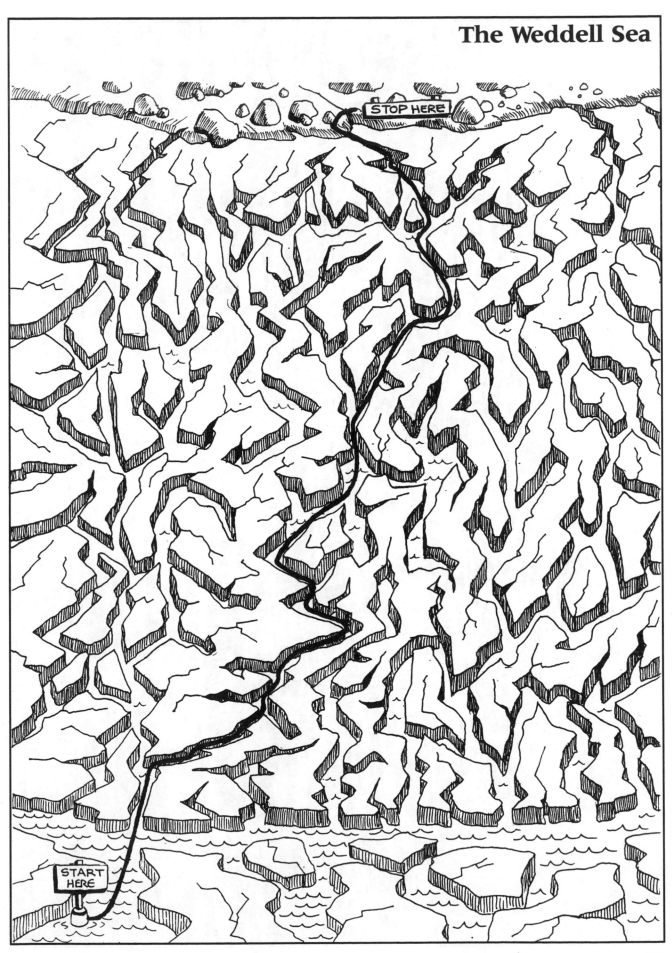

The Weddell Sea

STOP HERE

START HERE

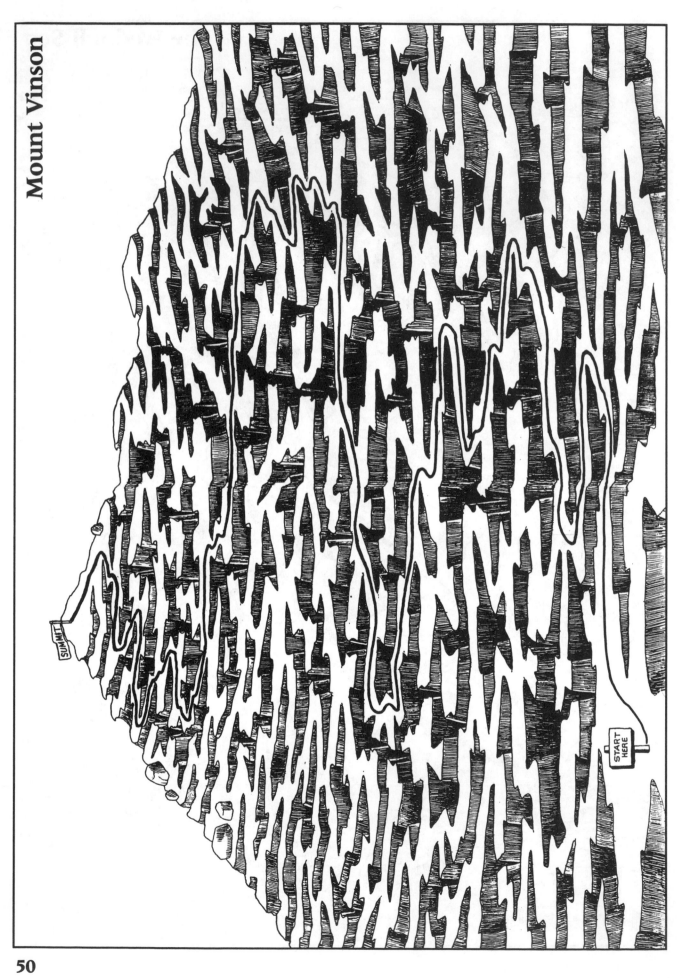

SUMMIT

START HERE

START HERE

STOP HERE

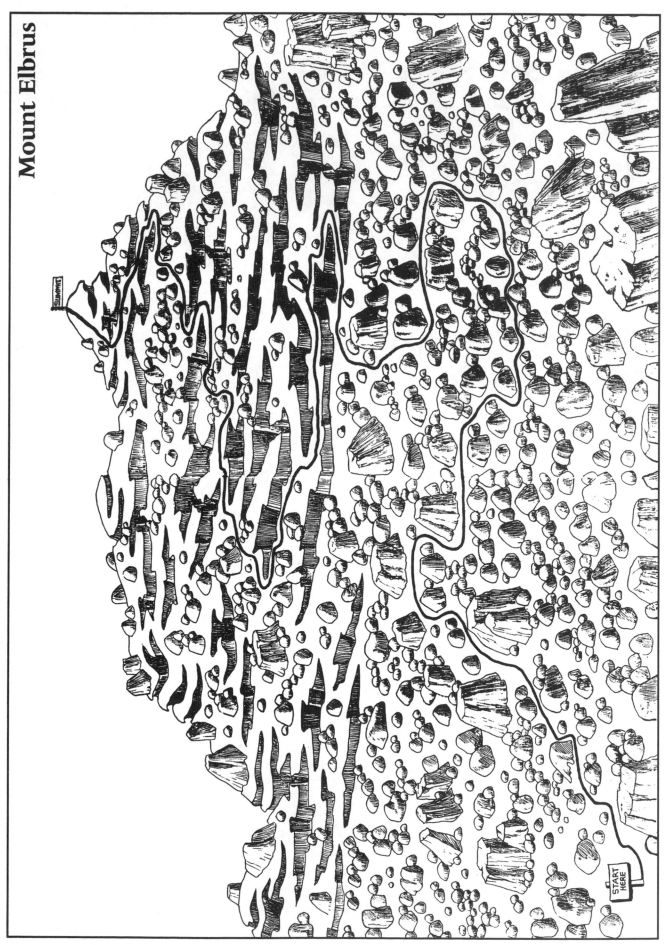

SUMMIT

START HERE

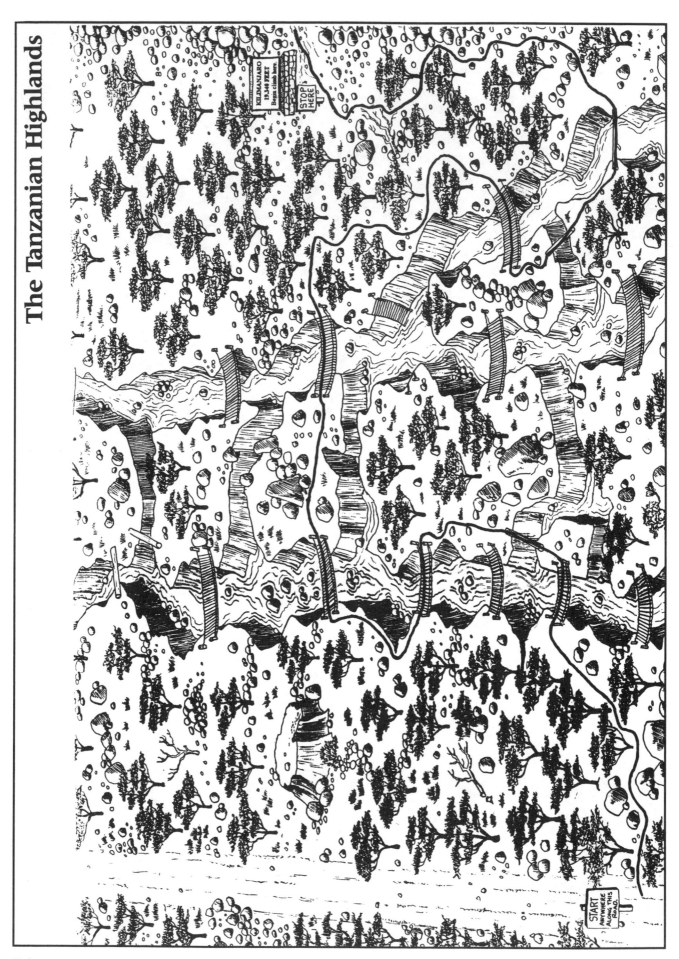

KILIMANJARO
19,340 FEET
Begin climb here.

STOP
HERE

START
ANYWHERE
ALONG THIS
ROAD.

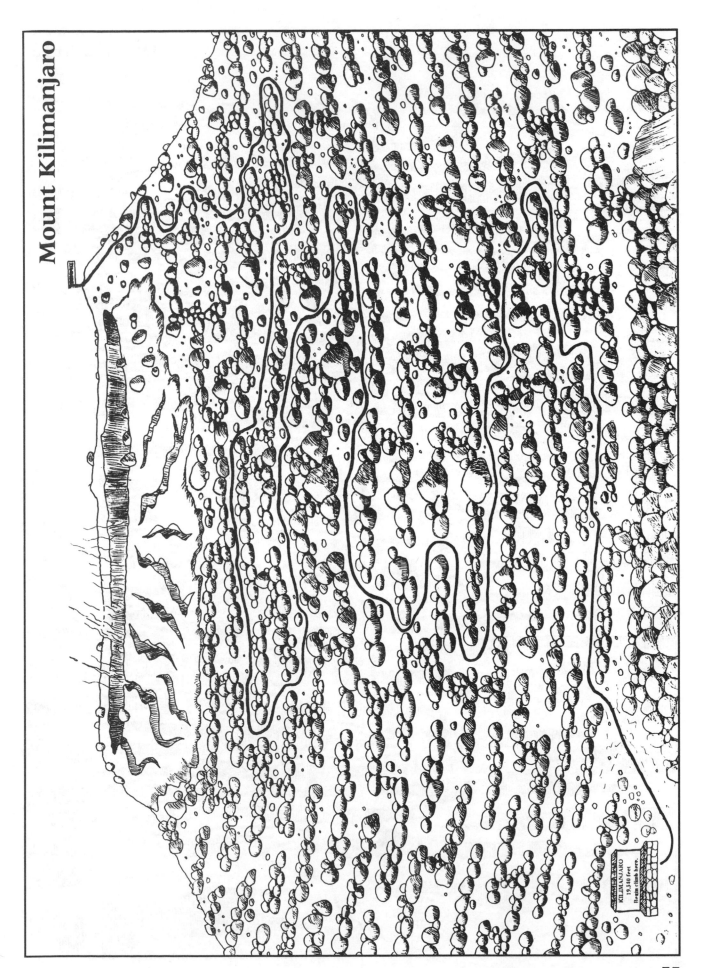

Mount Kilimanjaro

KILIMANJARO
19,340 feet
Begin climb here.

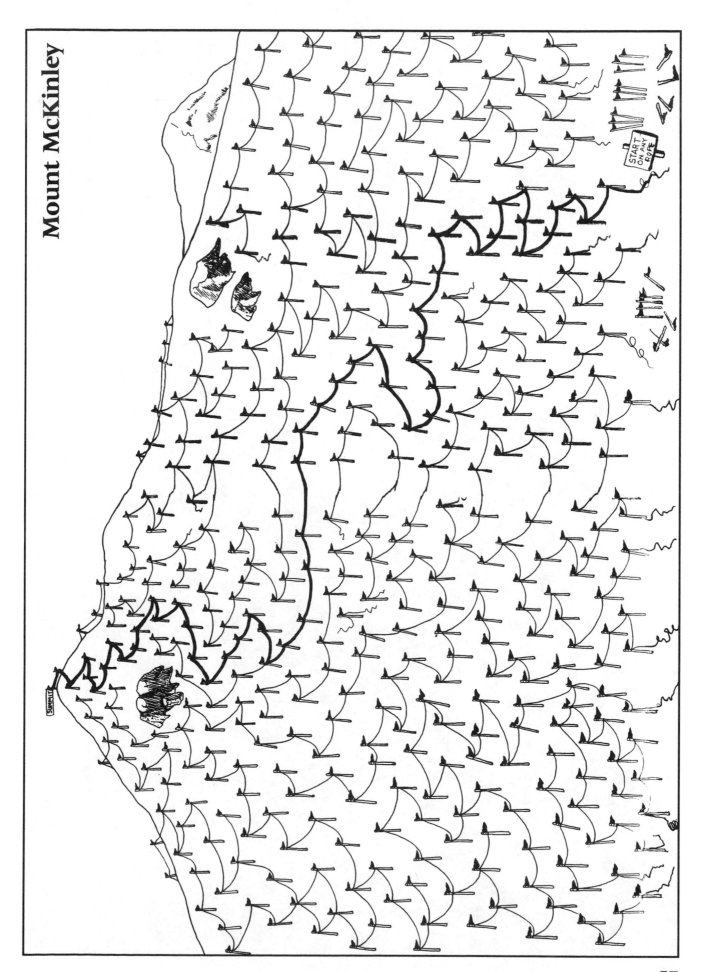

Mount McKinley

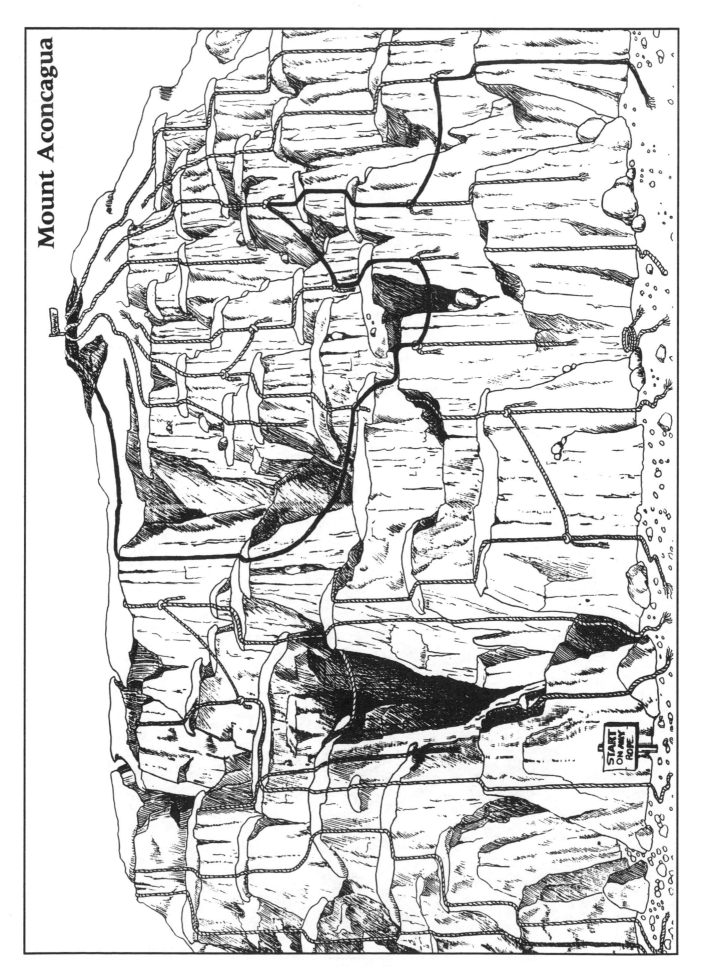

Mount Aconcagua

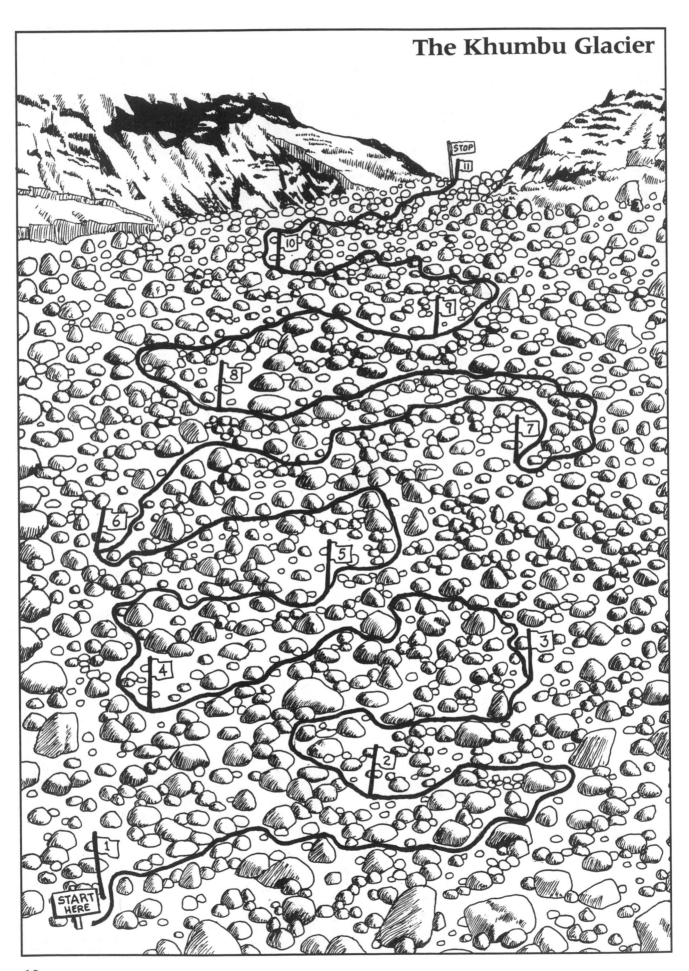

The Khumbu Glacier

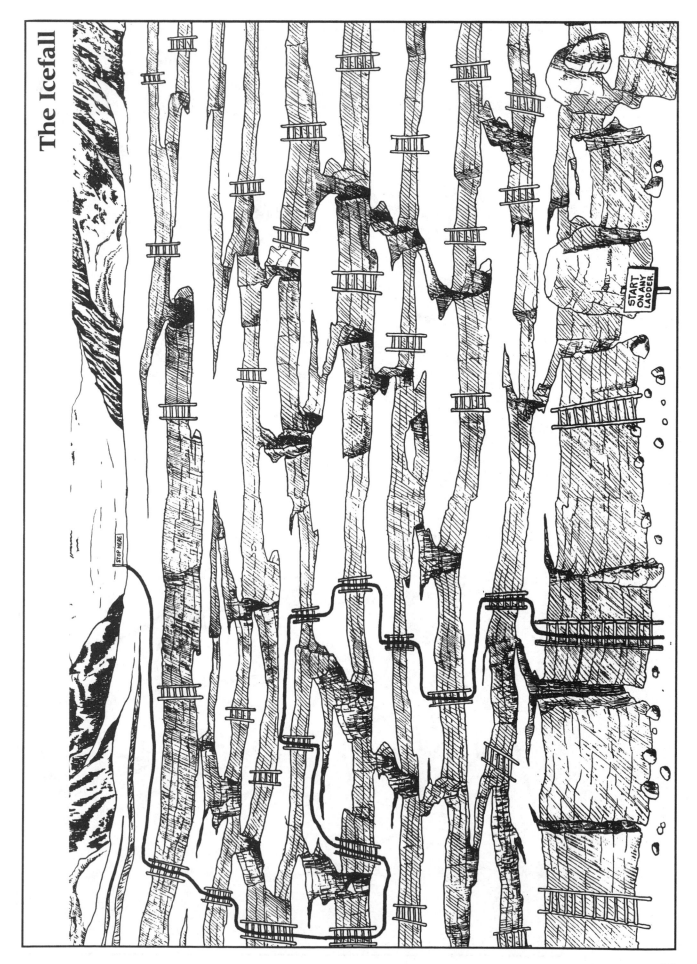

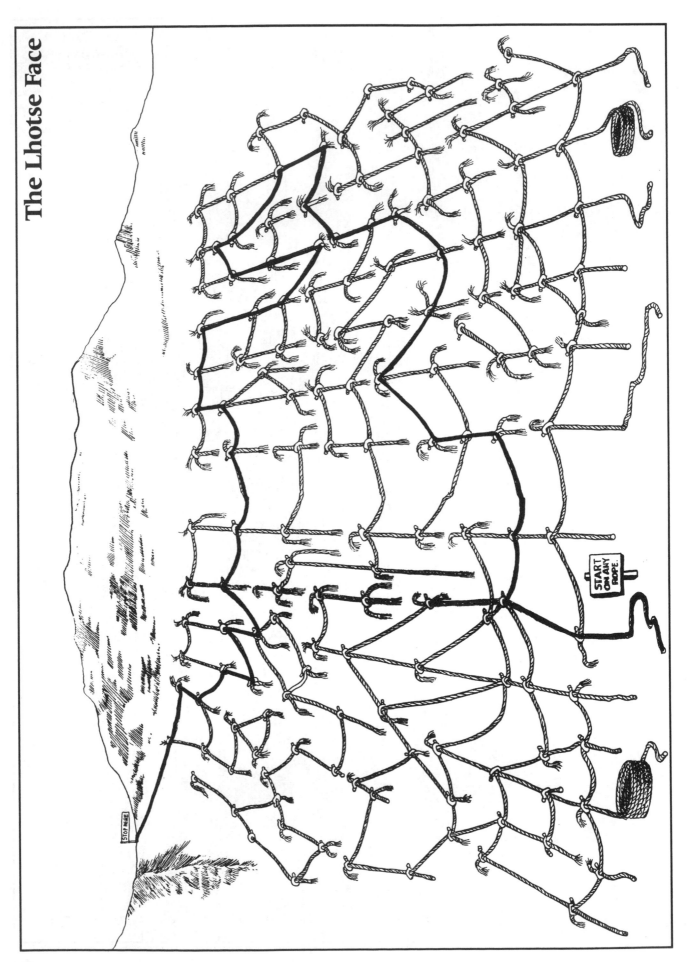

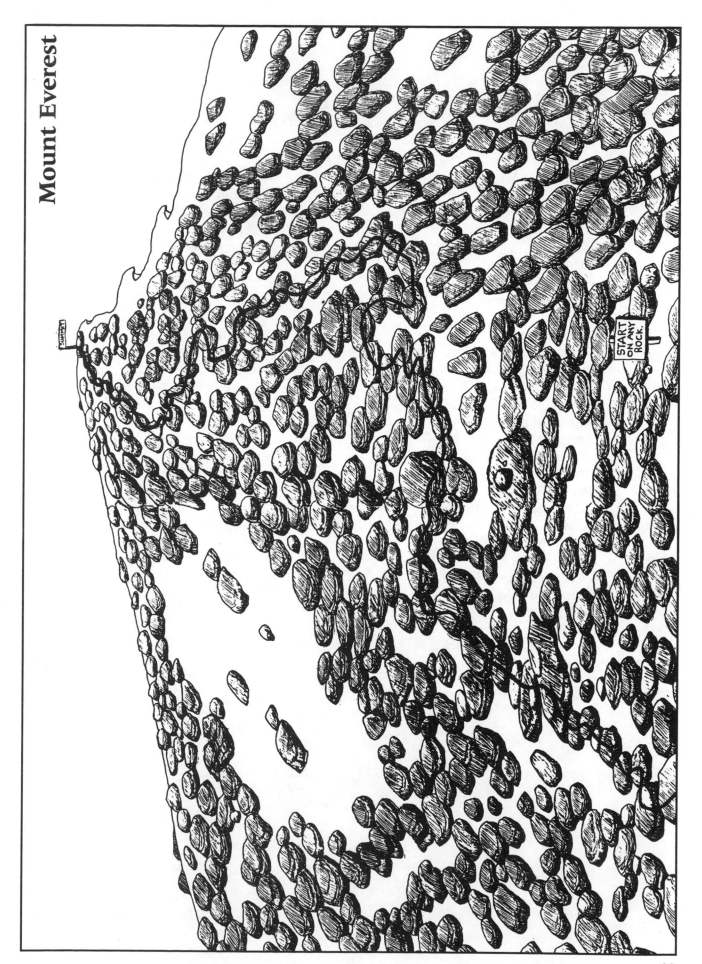

SUMMIT

START
ON ANY
ROCK.

INDEX

Climbing Guides are indicated by italics.